CW00760825

Cute
land

I LOVE KAWAII

First published in 2011 by
Harper Design
An Imprint of HarperCollins*Publishers*
10 East 53rd Street
New York, NY 10022
Tel: (212) 207-7000
Fax: (212) 207-7654
harperdesign@harpercollins.com
www.harpercollins.com

Distributed throughout the world by
HarperCollins*Publishers*
10 East 53rd Street
New York, NY 10022
Fax: (212) 207-7654

Editor and project director:
Josep Mª Minguet

Selection and art director:
Charuca

Design by:
Rubén García Cabezas

Translation by:
Babyl Traducciones

ISBN: 978-0-06-208282-4

Library of Congress Control Number 2011932416

Printed in China
First Printing, 2011

Selected by Charuca

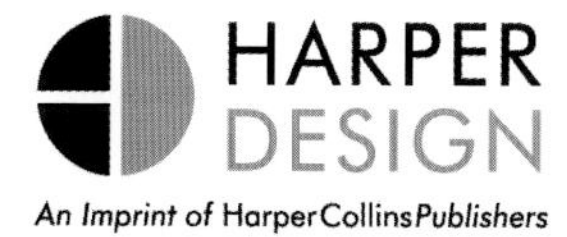

An Imprint of HarperCollins*Publishers*

charuca®

CONTENTS

I LOVE KAWAII: INTRODUCTION

Kawaii is a Japanese word meaning "adorable, sweet, cute." It's common for the Japanese to exclaim, "Kawaiiiiii!!!" upon seeing something or someone that is exceptionally cute—a puppy, kitten, or baby, for example. Kawaii can also apply to anything that appears childish, both in terms of an object's graphic simplicity— geometrical and curved shapes and bright colors—and the humorous and/or positive message it conveys. Another feature of kawaii is that everything, be it object or animal, is humanized. The proportion between head and body is extremely distorted. A kawaii character usually has a head the same size as the rest of the body, sometimes even larger. Think of the world-famous Japanese icon Hello Kitty—the perfect global example of kawaii.

I had wanted to put together a book on kawaii art for some time. At the risk of sounding like a kawaii freak, I have to admit that I am a huge fan of the art. My love for it borders on the obsessive. Not only have I integrated some aspects of kawaii into my own artwork, but I have also sought out the best kawaii artists in the field to learn from them. Aside from this, being the compulsive collector of art books that I am, I could no longer stand the gap in my bookcase, which desperately needed filling with a collection on this type of art. After a great deal of research, I decided to create this book myself, presenting works of my own as well as those of my favorite artists. I felt an urgent need to share kawaii with the rest of the world if only to make life a little more pleasant and enjoyable. I want you to fall in love with kawaii just as I have.

The book you are holding in your hands is a whimsical compendium of kawaii-based creations from a handful of my favorite artists, many of whom are my friends. Each artist, of course, has his/her own unmistakable style. This book celebrates the art of kawaii—and the artists who are at the cusp of the form—for all its color, supercute graphics, and delightful sense of humor. I think these images are incredibly exciting; they carry me away to a dream world filled with bright colors and the sweet smell of candy.

I welcome you to my kawaii world, and hope you enjoy your trip.

p8
PANDA SEA

p9
T-shirt design

CLAPPING HANDS

ARANZI ARONZO
Osaka, Japan
www.aranziaronzo.com
tokyo@aranziaronzo.com

ARONZO

In 1991, Yoko Yomura and Kinuyo Saito created the brand Aranzi Aronzo. Their premise is quite simple: "To create and sell the sort of things we like." Yomura and Saito began by creating fabric dolls in their homes and selling them in shops. Aranzi Aronzo currently employs twenty staff members and makes all types of products; each product is treated and created with love. Aranzi Aronzo puts quality before quantity and any product bearing this name is vigorously inspected for quality control. Aranzi characters are unmistakable: They have a captivating style with some highly amusing graphics. Their shop in Daikanyama, Tokio, is well worth a visit.

p10
WHITE RABBIT BROWN BUNNY

p11
T-shirt design

White Rabbit Brown Bunny

ARaNzo

Bubi
AuYeung

MILKJAR.COM

Bubi was born and grew up in Hong Kong where she worked as a multimedia professional by day and a passionate illustrator by night. She has always enjoyed drawing, reading comics, and collecting dolls. In 2004, she became a freelance illustrator, creating a series of stories drawn with her own characters. "Treeson," her most famous character, was born on August 8, 2005. This character has a marshmallow-like body and a stem branching out of his heart. (But don't worry, he's not in pain.) Bubi is a highly respected artist on the kawaii scene. Her work is simply adorable—the embodiment of kawaii.

BUBI AU YEUNG
Hong Kong, China
www.milkjar.com
bubi@milkjar.com

p14
Treeson illustrations

p15
Treeson illustrations

Sweden calling!

bukubuku

Having closely witnessed the artistic development of my friend Silvia Portella Torres, otherwise known as Bukubuku, I feel particularly fond of her work. I first met Silvia in Barcelona. Thanks to her, I discovered the city's most popular kawaii spots. Silvia has been working within the origins of kawaii illustration and has finally been given free reign. The result is a collection of some extremely sweet characters, who live in a unique setting—a visual mash-up, perhaps, of her birthplace Barcelona and the city of Berlin, where she has now lived for some years. Her creations can be seen in numerous German publications as well as in the form of some very tasty products on sale in her shops in Etsy or Poketo.

BUKUBUKU
Berlin, Germany
www.hellobukubuku.wordpress.com
bukubuku@gmx.de

Happy Donut
Daily made
ToFu House

The Superhero Store
FRUiT MARKET

p20
KNITTING TIME

POKETO WALLET 1

p21
OUR FAVORITE TREE

p22
ZWILLINGE

p23
BLOWN AWAY

COMÍA

CATALINA ESTRADA

Catalina Estrada has a spirit full of light. This is what I felt the first time I visited one of her exhibitions at the Iguapop Gallery. It was there the arrow struck and with it my unconditional love for this Columbian artist, the indefatigable worker now settled in Barcelona. Catalina and her art are one. Light, beauty, a message of hope, and another of criticism. Small birds and deer live together with bloodthirsty wolves. They are part of the same life. Catalina combines her artistic projects with commercial ones as long as they have an influence on her accessories and lifestyle products. She also works on photography and illustration projects with her husband Pancho Tolchinsky.

CATALINA ESTRADA
Barcelona, Spain
www.catalinaestrada.com
catiestrada@gmail.com

p24
LITTLE RED RIDING HOOD
Vector illustration

p25
MOTHERLAND
Vector illustration

p26
BIRD
Published in *Computer Arts* magazine
Vector illustration

p27
UNICEF: LOVE IS ALL
For UNICEF
Vector illustration

...LOVE IS ALL...
CATALINA·ESTRADA

I ♥ KAWAII
かわいい
かわいい
かわいい
かわいい
かわいい
charuca

I am absolutely delighted to be able to share some of my work with you. In my gallery you can see Megamoder, my first collection of characters, which can also be seen on the Web site Mondotrendy.com. There were many more characters to come after Megamoder. I love each and every one of the characters I've created; they are my children! I also have a great deal of love for my BBZ toy collection, something I created jointly with Kachingbrands in 2007. I believe there's nothing more exciting for a character designer than to see their creature in the palm of their hand. The very first time I saw the BBZ prototypes I was almost in tears!

CHARUCA
Barcelona, Spain
www.charuca.net
charuca@charuca.net

CHARUCA STICKERS. Diseñadas con mucho cariño para todos los amantes de las cosas bonitas *(^_^)*
hello (again)
charuca
www.charuca.net
caca
Cute land
email me!
Cute
© Charuca, 2008 · All rights reserved · www.charuca.net · charuca@charuca.net

p30
CHARUCA STICKER SHEET
For *BG* magazine, n.29. Ecuador

p31
CHARUCA PANG
For the book *Designers' Games RMX*, UBER BOOKS, Germany

COBI WORLD
Cobi's homage exhibiton by Duduá in Barcelona

LOS MEGAMODER
First Internet characters by Charuca

MIAM MIAM

Clémentine

p32
MISH MASH BURGER
Illustrations for the video Mish Mash Burger directed by Bupla

p33
BURGER
Character design for the video Mish Mash Burger directed by Bupla

p34–35
EASTER
Illustration for a game published in *Charlotte aux Fraixes* magazine

p36–37
CHARACTER DESIGN MIX
Promotional card

For years I have been enchanted by the work of French artist Clémentine Derodit—smiling cherries and a milk bottle, which doubles as a baby panda. Clémentine has worked as a freelance designer since 2002 along with Mathieu Quiblier in the Bupla pool. The majority of her work consists of illustrations for children's magazines. She is also about to publish her first illustrated book titled *Et toque!*, which will be published by Marchand de feuilles Edition.

CLÉMENTINE
Lyon, France
www.bupla.com
clementine.derodit@free.fr

SIROP
S

Devils have
Cuteness and Little Blackness
CAPSULE
ROBOT
01
colette
©2009 DEVILROBOTS [TO-FU OYAKO] ©2009 DEVILROBOTS / GREENCAMEL [evirob] ©2009 DEVILROBOTS / MEDICOM TOY

devil robots

Devilrobots is a studio in Tokyo, Japan. From a place crammed full of dolls and all types of pop items, Shinishiro Kitaii, the studio's art director, is effectively a dispenser of kawaii characters. The studio specializes in the creation of graphics, characters, illustrations, animation, Web sites, and music. I have to confess I feel a certain predilection for Shinishiro and Devilrobots. Their characters require no introduction. You may already be familiar with their most famous character, To-Fu Oyako, a product featured in countless specialized design shops.

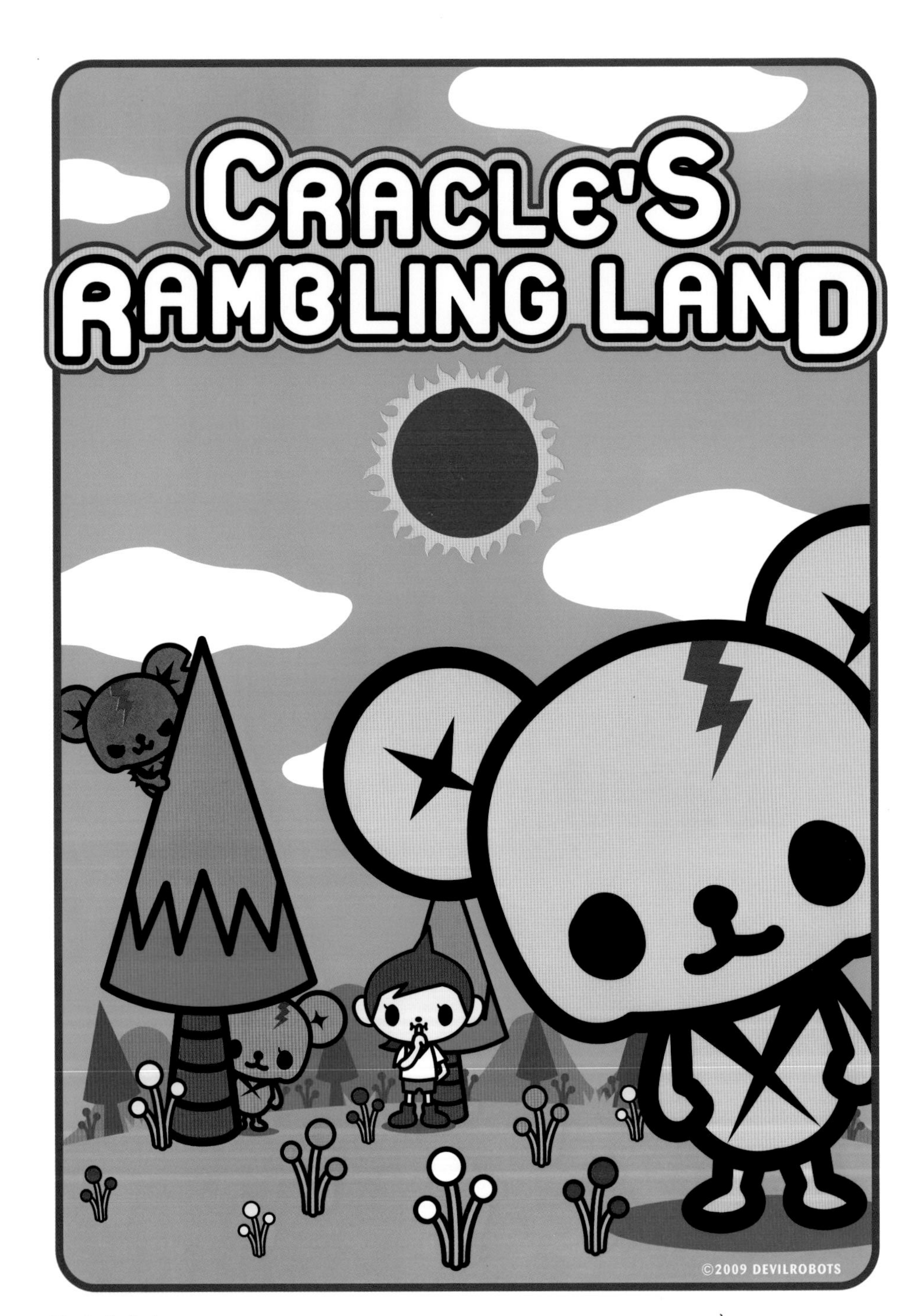
CRACLE'S
RAMBLING LAND
©2009 DEVILROBOTS

JAPAN
TO-FU OYAKO
©2009 DEVILROBOTS / GREENCAMEL

ALICE IN WONDERLAND

Designed by DEVILROBOTS

DRINK ME

p42
ALICE IN WONDERLAND

p43
ALICE IN WONDERLAND

Douman's illustrations are 100 percent kawaii, in the broadest sense of the term. Douman also has the indisputable Japanese touch, which stems from the most classic kawaii. Small, smiling animals, very childish illustrations, small rounded shape—nobody can resist saying,"Ahhhhh!" Douman says she is good at doing humorous illustrations and that she would like to illustrate amusing stories of interest to people. She is currently working as an illustrator for magazine and book publishers, Web sites, and advertising firms.

DOUMAN
Japan
www.doumanworld.com
dmankazu@ybb.ne.jp

p48
ANIMALS 1

p49
ANIMALS 2

WOOHOO

TA
LAA
LA TA LA

LUCK

Miami

Friends™
WITH YOU
♥ XLR8R

BOOPY

The End

p50
Illustration for *Xlr8r* magazine

p51
WISH COME TRUE
Toy collection
Produced by Strange CO

Friends With You is an artistic collaborative based in Miami, Florida, and founded by artists Samuel Borkson and Arturo Sandoval. Since 2002, FWY have been endorsing their message of magic, luck, and friendship, these being the core concepts the artists communicate through their collections of art toys and installations, and advertising campaigns. Their style is characterized by a minimalist approach to design and an explosion of primary colors, nearly always balanced with white. Best of all? FWY want to be your friends!

FRIENDSWITHYOU
Miami, USA
www.friendswithyou.com
info@friendswithyou.com

p52
KAWAII CHARACTERS

MALFIPANORAMA 2

p53
FRIENDSWITHYOU HAVE POWERS
Book cover

LOVE SEEN

p54–55
FUN FUN

p56–57
WISH COME TRUE

Friends With You

ends

Friends™
WITH YOU

WISH
COME
TRUE

©Hiroko Yokoyama

p58
HAPPY LOVERS

p59
STRAWBERRY GIRL

In the words of Hiroko Yokohama, the self-taught Japanese illustrator, the driving force behind her creations is to think about what makes people happy. Happiness—this is exactly what I felt when I came across Hiroko's Web site whilst making one of my habitual kawaii excursions. Her illustrations generate this feeling of well-being, something that is achieved by only the finest kawaii artists. Her style is extremely feminine and the quality of her illustrations is exceptional; the finish and the use of color are absolutely impeccable.

HIROKO YOKOYAMA
Kagawa, Japan
www.yokoyama-hiroko.com
hirorin@yokoyama-hiroko.com

p60
THE CROWN OF WHITE CLOVER

p61
THE TIME OF THE MILK

THE LOVERS' ST.VALENTINE'S DAY

Hiroko
Yokoyama

CHU
LOVE
Happy Valentine
Hiroko Yokoyama

Cutie
Mermaid
Hiroko Yokoyama

p62
CUTIE MERMAID

p63
I AM PETER PAN

THE RAINBOW THAT RAIN RAISES

Itokin Park.

p64
FROG

p65
MINAZUKIN (MOON BOY)
Vinyl toy

p66–67
LUCHA BEAR
Character design

Itokin Park©

I came across the work of Kazuhiko Ito, otherwise known as Itokin Park, thanks to a collection of Fimo dolls I discovered on the Internet. What struck me about her work was the juxtaposition of modern and retro design, which Kazuhiko applies to all of her characters, together with their soft and asymmetrical shapes. After this set of dolls, many others followed, which have achieved international fame. Her little characters stand out for their excellent artistic appeal. Itokin Park produces limited editions of pieces, which are extremely difficult to get hold of, much to the delight of the most fervent collectors.

ITOKIN PARK
Japan
www.itokin-park.com
kazuhiko@itokin-park.com

Lucha Bear
Presented by Itokin Park http://www.itokin-park.com

Lucha Bear
Presented by Itokin Park http://www.itokin-park.com

p68
REINVENT LETOY
Illustration for Letoy

p69
YOGA BUNNY
Personal artwork

Laura Osorno is a well-known Columbian artist living in New York City, where she is currently fulfilling her dream of creating characters, clothing, accessories, and all types of lovely, kawaii-oriented products. She has a very individual style: naive illustrations with an extremely bright color palette and clean lines. I myself was moved by all of Laura's characters. I particularly fell in love with her drawing of a little rabbit afraid to go out on the street. The fact is that in Laura's world nothing is as simple as it looks.

LAURA OSORNO
Colombia
www.lauraosorno.net
lauraosorno@gmail.com

p70
ROBE, LOLA AND MAX
Illustration for *MDI* magazine

MY EYES ADORE YOU
Personal artwork

TEENAGER

CHARACTERS STUDY
Personal artwork

MIA
Personal artwork

p71
MIS 3 JUEGOS FAVORITOS
Published in a collective magazine

I LOVE JAPAN
Personal artwork

p72
CHARACTERS STUDY A
Personal artwork

CHARACTERS STUDY B
Personal artwork

p73
SUPERMERCADO
Published in a collective magazine

supermercado

p74
HEY!
Personal artwork

p75
OMEGA 3

NIÑA PULPO
Record cover

MEETING THE PARENTS

Espinosa

p76
SILENT KISSES
Self promotion illustration

p77
CAPITÁN OREJAS
Character study for an upcoming graphic novel

p78
SCOOTER BUG
Handbag design illustration created for Littleheart designer series

WEEHEE!
Personal artwork

p79
KIKO
Character design

SCOOTER BUG
Handbag design illustration created for Littleheart designer series

Leo Espinosa is a Colombian artist currently living in Cambridge, Massachusetts. Most of his kawaii illustrations have a highly personal style, a certain sweetness that only a person with Leo's sensitivity is capable of achieving. My favorite characters are Otis and Rae. The design, the shapes, and the choice of colors simply drive me crazy. The composition is highly entertaining. Leo combines his artistic projects with more commercial projects, such the animation for Sushi Pack and various publicity campaigns or incursions in the licensing world, such as the wide range of products he has jointly created with Coca-Cola.

LEO ESPINOSA
Cambridge, USA
www.studioespinosa.com
leo@studioespinosa.com

Espinosa

kiko
kiko
kiko

p80
OTIS AND RAE
Design and development for a multi-platform property
launched as a children's book titled *Otis and Rae and the Grumbling Splunk*

p81
DICEKAY
Opener for the sports section of the *Boston Globe* welcoming
Daisuke Matsuzaka, aka Dice-Kay, to the Boston Red Sox baseball team

グリーンモンスター
ゴーソックス

Espinosa

apple sauce
NATURALLY SWEET
NO SUGAR ADDED!

p82–83
KRIS KROS APPLESAUCE
Character and product design
for a licensing property

p84
SNOW WHITE

p85
T-shirt design

Lilidoll is a Parisian artist whose sweet and splendid illustrations I find enchanting. Lilidoll characters appear innocent at first glance, but anyone who takes a little time to delve inside their world will discover that there is a dark power behind these stubborn, retro-like creatures. I just love the Lilidoll figures; not only is Lilidoll's attention to detail evident, but so is the care she takes to create them. Aside from her work in advertising and publications, native and foreign, Lilidoll also merchandises T-shirts, dolls, and all sorts of desirable objects.

LILIDOLL
Nantes, France
www.lilidoll.com
lilidoll_power@yahoo.fr

p86
THORN FOREST

p87
GREEN BIRD

p88
MINA

p89
CHARACTER BORARD

JE GRIBOUILLE AU JARDIN
Coloring diary (stationery)
for La Marelle Publisher (cover)

zz...

je gribouille au jardin
Avec mes couleurs !
Ma peinture !
Mes feutres !

little ★ Amie

BORINGGGGGG ...

p90
"LITTLE-AMIE" FIGURE

p91
AMIE

ahtam ♥ TAM

It was in Atticus BCN, one of Barcelona's best toyshops, where I first came across a piece by Little Amie. I was astonished by the infinite sweetness of one character in particular, who was sleeping in a cup. I found myself being careful not to wake her. I arrived home determined to learn more about the creator and this was how I got to know about Little Amie's world. I discovered that hidden behind this name there was an artist who lived in Hong Kong. Nature, animals, and the unexpected achievements in everyday life are her source of inspiration. Her philosophy is to create dreams and provide beauty in a world that clearly needs it.

LITTLE AMIE
Hong Kong
www.little-amie.com
ahtam.tam@gmail.com

p92
LITTLE AMIE DOODLE

p92–93
Designs for Megabox box

Ok!
Please use energy saving bulb!

p94
"LITTLE-AMIE" FIGURE

p95
"AMIE-RABBIT" FIGURE

little ★ Amie

little ★ Amie
copyright © ahtamTAM all rights reserved.

p96
FLOWERPOT
T-shirt design

p97
THE TUMMIEFRIENDS
Adventures on Sugarhill

p98–99
THE TUMMIEFRIENDS
Adventures on Sugarhill

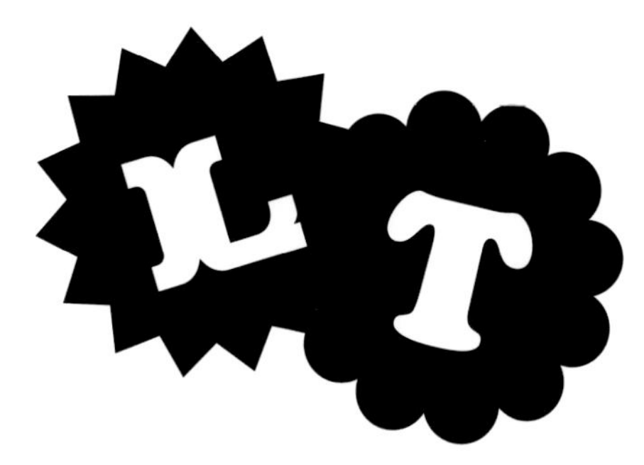

LOULOU & TUMMIE

LouLou & Tummie is a Dutch illustration studio that aims to expand its empire of characters and multicolored graphics. They create whole kawaii-inspired worlds and illustrations for magazines, books, advertising, and interiors. Their art can appear as decorative wall designs or in the form of adorable soft dolls and accessories. They have just brought out The Tummie Friends, a brand of adorable products launched at the Taipei Toy Festival.

LOULOU & TUMMIE
Tilburg, The Netherlands
www.loulouandtummie.com
info@loulouandtummie.com

Miss Fruitcake

the Tummie Friends
Sugarhill

p100
SATURDAY NIGHT MARI-CHAN

p101
MARI-CHAN
Charcater design

CHARACTERS

MARI-CHAN

Mari Chan was one of the first kawaii artists I came across. It was way back in 2002 when little Terelo provided me with a Web link that opened the door to the world of Masanori Handa, otherwise known as Mari Chan. Born in Osaka, Japan, Mari says it is her intention to express her feelings through her work. Despite their sometimes serious outward manner, the Japanese are full of happy surprises, as Mari herself proves. Her world is bold and playful and devoid of any sense of artistic restriction.

MARI-CHAN
Tokyo, Japan
www.marichan.com
marichanps@gmail.com

マリちゃん

CONGRATULATIONS

わんぱく
日記

p102
BIKKURI BANG

p103
POSTCARDS

p104–105
CHARACTERS

p106
RAINY SEASON

p107
MARI-CHAN THEME

p108
CLOUD MUSIC

p110–111
THE CLOUD SEEDERS

meomi

www.meomi.com

Meomi is the dream factory created by Vancouver-based Vicki Wong and L.A.-based Michael Murphy.Their work has been reviewed in countless books, design magazines, and e-zines. Their graphics are super sweet and include everything from simple compositions to extremely elaborate and highly detailed works. And, as if this weren't enough, these artists are completely committed to spreading kawaii around the world. They were responsible for designing the adorable mascots for the Vancouver 2010 Olympic Games and regularly publish illustrated books for both children and adults.

MEOMI
Vancouver, Canada
www.meomi.com
info@meomi.com

THE
CLOUD
SEEDERS
© MEOMI DESIGN INC. 2008

p112
SHADY TEA

p113
JELLY FISH

p114–115
SUMMER

THE OCTONAUTS

© MIMIO CLUB 2009
LUCKY MAIL
ARE YOU MERRY ME ?
I AM MOMO
I AM CHICHI
BLACK PING
I AM DAPAN
CRAZY MAIL
SWORDSMAN
ROCK CHICKEN
BEATIFIC MAIL
CRAZY TO YOU
GO TO PLAY
GO TO THE PARTY
BEATIFIC TO YOU
I AM TOMATO
I LOVE SUMMER
I LOVE CHECKER
I LOVE FLOWER
FUNNY TO YOU
DO YOU HAPPY ?
I AM HURT
CHINA
Confucius's Classroom
I LOVE CHINA
I NEED LOVE
COOL
CALL ME COWBOY
LUCKY TO YOU
FUNNY MAIL
I AM KING IN THE WORLD
RED PING
JANPAN DREAM
Mimio's
Friends
I AM MIMIO
I AM ELFI
I AM MANI
I AM AHA
MIMIO
MIMIO BELIEVE, WE CAN MAKE A PRETTY WORLD.
LUCKY GIRL
WWW.MIMIOCLUB.COM

p116
MIMIOFRIENDS SHOW

p117
LUCKY JANE

Maxpipi believes that we can build a beautiful world. Mimio is the name of the main character on the Web by Maxpipi, an artist resident in Taipei, Taiwan. Her work is simply impeccable. Maxpipi completely masters the art of kawaii illustration. Her vectors are perfect. Mimio exists alongside other incredibly sweet characters such as Aha, Elfu, and Mani, and, as if this weren't enough, each one has its own mascot. It's a kawaii paradise.

MAXPIPI
Taipei, Taiwan
www.mimioclub.com
pipi@mimioclub.com

© MIMIO CLUB 2008 / WWW.MIMIOCLUB.COM
MIMIO
BEAUTY

MIMIO
BEAUTY
MIMIO
BEAUTY
24
BLOCKING
protective and moisturizing series
HOURS
SUPER CUTE
Always Beautiful, Always Mimio Beauty!
Will Never Go Out Of Style

p118–119
MIMIO MAGAZINE CONTENTS
Brand image advertisement in a magazine
concerning a fictitious cosmetic brand

p120
MIMIO AND MOMO

AHA AND CHICHI

p121
MANI AND DAPAN

ELFU AND TOMATO

roporopo

pouly*

I am pouly. I am piggy.
I like beautiful, lovely things.

p122
POULY

p123
WHITE BEAR

mizuka

We return to the land of the rising sun to present the intricate work of this Tokyo-based artist. Mizuka began as a freelance illustrator in 2006, specializing in the design of little animals and kawaii characters. As is usually the case with Japanese artists, Mizuka has created a unique line of illustrated objects and has also published children's books. I just love the way she makes use of retro-like aesthetics from the 1950s and 1960s. She is one of the few Japanese artists who has distanced themselves from the classic kawaii to adopt a more Western approach.

MIZUKA
Tokyo, Japan
www.mizuka-web.com
info@mizuka-web.com

roporopo
Let's color the wall.

GO GO bicycle!!
There is a sky I can recommend.
The smell of the sky refreshes.
roporopo world
mizuka

RAINY DAY
roporopo

Smell of coffee.
It settles down when a good smell is smelt.
roporopo

p124
PAINTER

GO GO BICYCLE

RAINY DAY

SMELL OF COFFEE

p125
MARKET

THANK YOU VERY MUCH

p126
HIGAMBANA

p127
ICHIGO

roporopo
©mizuka

p128
CAMPTRAIT
T-shirt design

p129
MONDOTRENDY CONTACT
Character design

p130
UNTITLED

PABURITO SALUD
Icon design

PABURITO MENDIGO
Icon design

P131
NIÑO CON MONSTRI

ISLA
T-shirt design

KARMANERD
T-shirt design

I have always been a great fan of Pablo Moreno. This illustrator, originally from La Mancha and now settled in Barcelona, Spain, is more than just a friend. Together with Pablo and whilst we were experimenting without any intention other than to enjoy ourselves on the MONDOTRENDY Web site, I discovered that my passion for illustration overrode the limits of the hobby. Pablo currently works as a freelance illustrator on projects for advertising agencies, as well as for publishers. Pablo's kawaii illustrations are adorable, sweet, and charming. His little rounded characters and his subtle sense of humor always bring a smile to my face.

PABLO MORENO
Barcelona, Spain
www.mondotrendy.com
info@mondotrendy.com

p132
DEEREST FRIENDS

p133
SKULLBOX

p134
RAINBOW KAIJU

CHERRY IS THE NEW BLOOD

p135
HOLLOW THREAT
Death Metal Legend character design

UNTITLED
Paper diorama

FIRST LADY
Paper diorama

Kawaii takes us to New Zealand, home of Paul Shih, who is originally from Taiwan. What struck me about Paul (apart from the indisputable quality of his graphics) was a technique he himself developed. This one-of-a-kind technique consists of combining illustration, paper cutting, and other photography techniques. The result is artwork entirely representative of Shih's sense of style and personality. According to Paul, by day he works as a freelance designer and illustrator and by night he locks himself away in his magic laboratory to conduct experiments with his creatures. He believes that one day his nocturnal characters will invade the earth. I'm convinced of it.

PAUL SHIH
Auckland, New Zealand
www.paul-shih.com
paul@paul-shih.com

EXIT

A

MR SNOUT

FABIAN

p136
BUTTER FACTORY - BUMP
Elements from wall art at
The Butter Factory in Singapore

p137
BUNNY & SPANNER
Editorial illustration

Peskimo is 50 percent by Jodie and 50 percent by David. They have been jointly creating creatures from Bristol, UK. Their characters have come into the world in the form of toys, animations, publicity products, and clothing for such as Kidrobot, Sony, Barclays, and Vodafone. Their inspiration comes from cartoons, vintage graphic design, chocolate, and spying on people at the post office. Their dream? To one day own an ice cream van.

PESKIMO
Bristol, United Kingdom
www.peskimo.com
go@peskimo.com

p138
SPLASH
Illustration for Moo.com

p139
VARIOUS CHARACTERS

p140
STEREO LOVE
Illustrated pattern

p141
HAPPY DROP AND SAD DROP
Illustrations for Moo.com

BUNNY BREATH - PREQUEL
Limited Gocco print for Kidrobot Dunny launch

p142
SUAVES COMO LA LANA
Pencil and Photoshop

p143
VERANO
Watercolor and ink

p144–145
BLACK & WHITE
Digital vector

Princesita is María Carrasco's alter ego. She was born in Málaga, Spain, in 1983 and, influenced by the stories her mother used to make up for her and her sisters, one day decided to be a princess and to create her own special world around her—a world where the girls come with curves, where color is fundamental, and where a free rein is given to anyone with the prettiest shoes. María is a hyperactive multidisciplinary artist, who exudes art through and through, in everything she does—from illustrations to the creation of a felt or fimo toy, slippers, or pretty little cakes.

LA PRINCESITA
Malaga, Spain
princesitastyle.com
laprincesita@princesitastyle.com

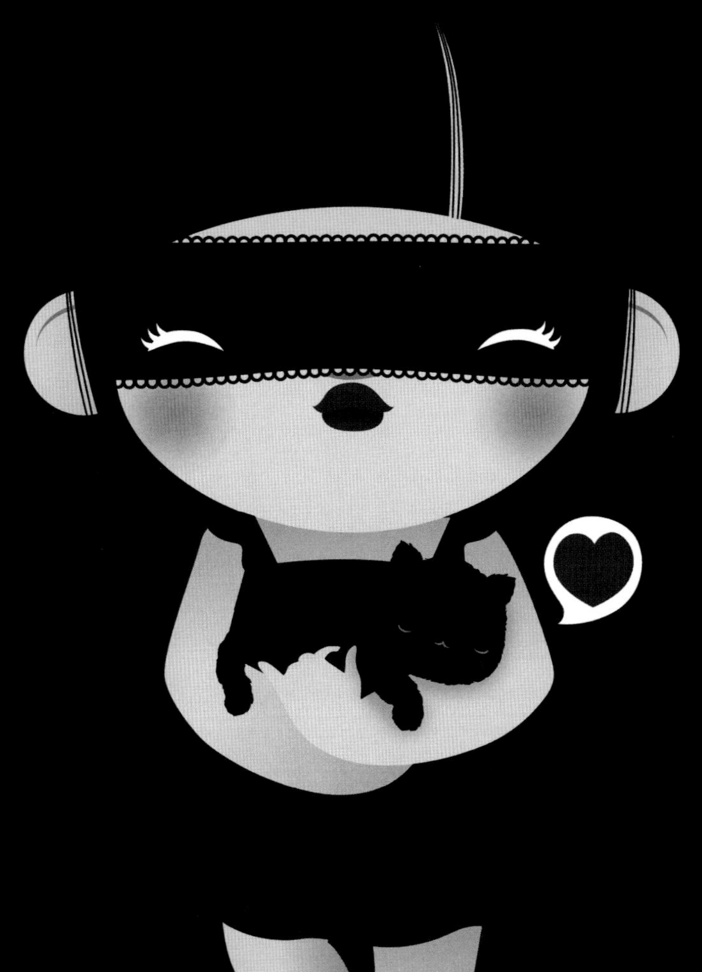
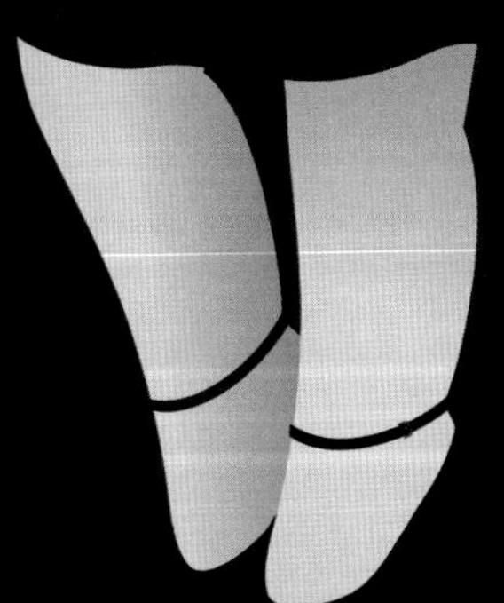

La Princesita

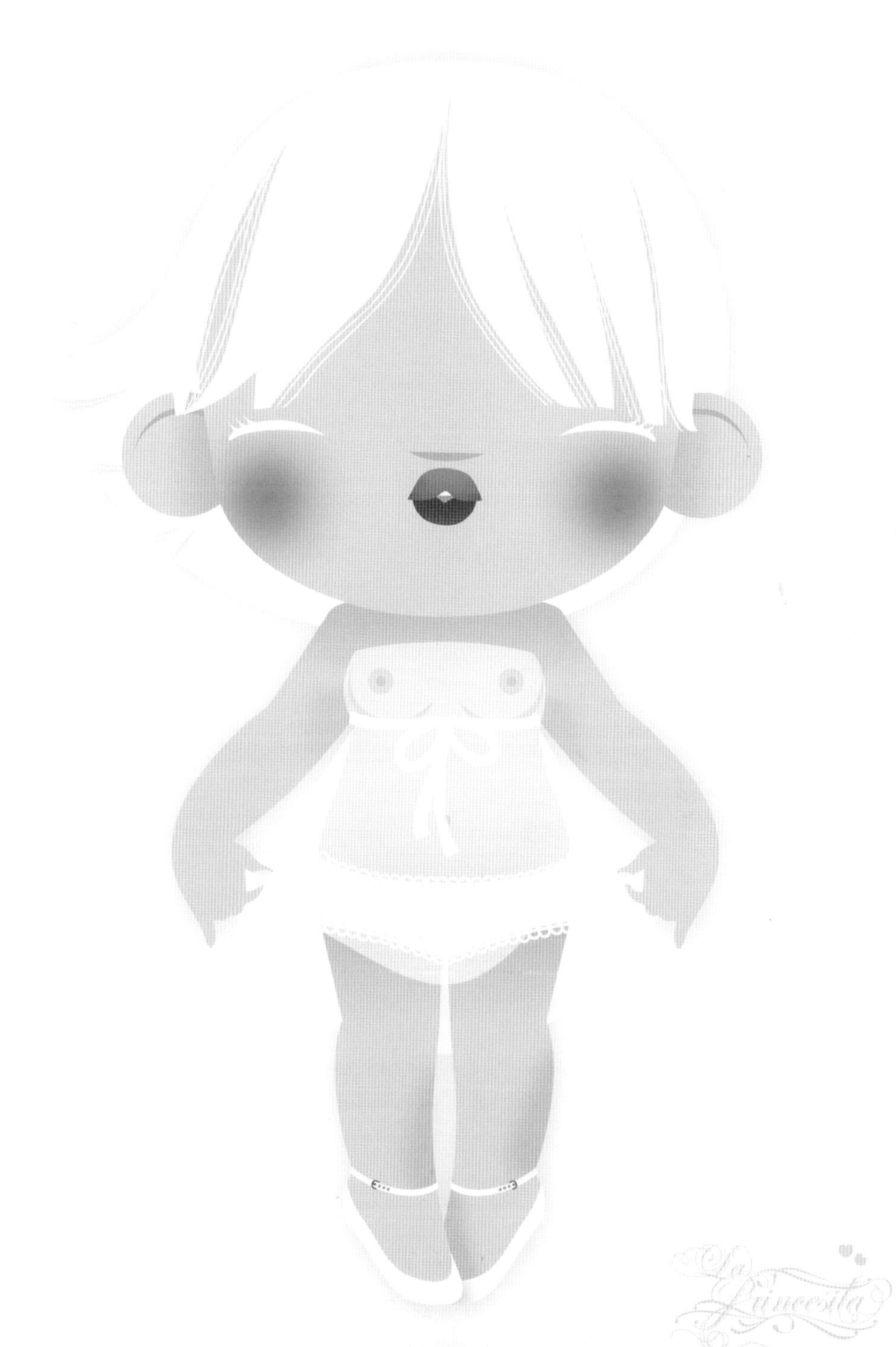
La Princesita

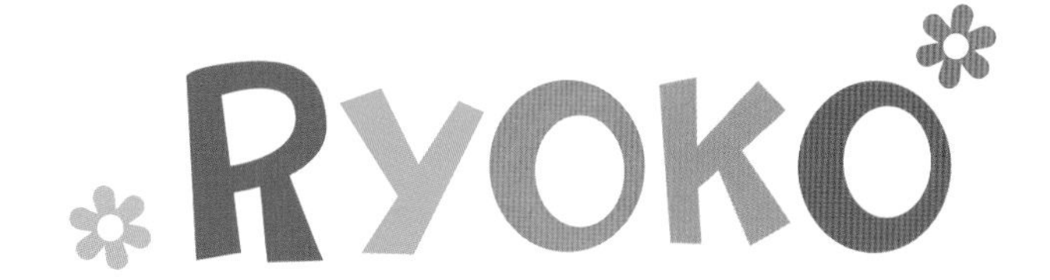

Ryoko is a Japanese artist living in Tokyo. She works as a freelance illustrator, and has also been developing her own kawaii-inspired world—a colorful place that abounds with unlimited happiness. Ryoka creates her own illustrated stories, which she also publishes. Her most artistic work consists of creating appealing graphics inspired by dreams. Her style is supercute and designed to make people happy. Her illustrations have recently been shown at the Artcomplex Center in Tokyo, Japan.

RYOKO
Tokyo, Japan
ryokooekaki.ciao.jp
ryoko-rk@excite.co.jp

Ryoko

Ryoko

Ryoko

Ryoko

p152
IN MY WORLD

Sheena Aw, otherwise known as Caramelaw, is a designer/illustrator from Singapore, China. Sheena specializes in motion graphics and her work includes designs for MTV Asia and Sony International. In 2005, she won a Promax Award for one of her promotions for MTV Asia. Her digital kawaii creations have made her well known all around the world. Sheena herself says if there's one thing she gets excited about it is being immersed in her world of sweets, rainbows, and mushrooms—a world of baroque kawaii compositions created entirely in vector mode.

SHEENA AW
Singapore
caramelaw.deviantart.com
mesourcream@yahoo.com

p154
DEPTHCORE HEIST

DEPTHCORE HER

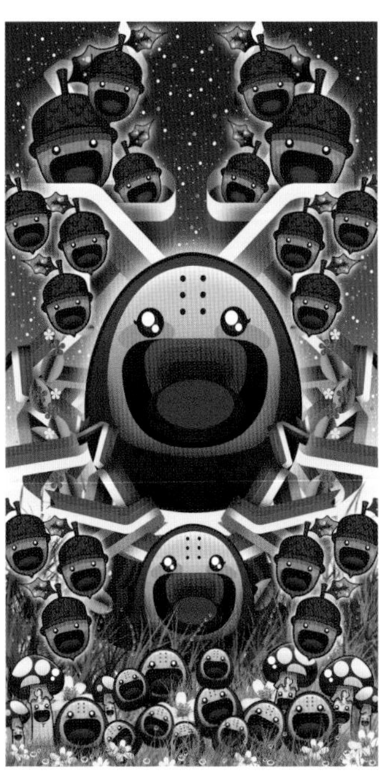

p155
DEPTHCORE MAJESTY

DEPTHCORE REQUIEM

!RESIST!
KEEP
SMILING

p156
RESIST
Poster

SUPER DEUX™

Sebastian Roux is the artist behind the brand Superdeux, which also happens to be the name of his design studio. This French artist, currently living in San Francisco, California, was one of the pioneers in working with a specific Japanese style of illustration in 2002. His style clearly has a Japanese influence; while his latest creations have a retro style language heavily dependent on graffiti culture, urban art, and electronic music. It could be said that Sebastian has had a great deal of influence on developing the most kawaii-orientated line, that of the art toy. He was certainly one of the first artists who went way beyond customizing a platform toy to have his own collection of characters, the most famous being the indisputably popular Stereotype.

SUPERDEUX
Lille, France
www.superdeux.com
info@superdeux.com

NO
SD

p158
MOODY SHOW 01

p159
MOODY SHOW 02

MOODY SHOW 03

KNOWLEDGE

kidrobot®
TADO
Fortune
PORK
Series 2

p160
FORTUNE PORK SERIES 2
Mini plush toys produced by Kidrobot 2009
www.kidrobot.com

p161
SUGAR BOMB
Wall vinyl mural produced by Domestic
www.domestic.fr

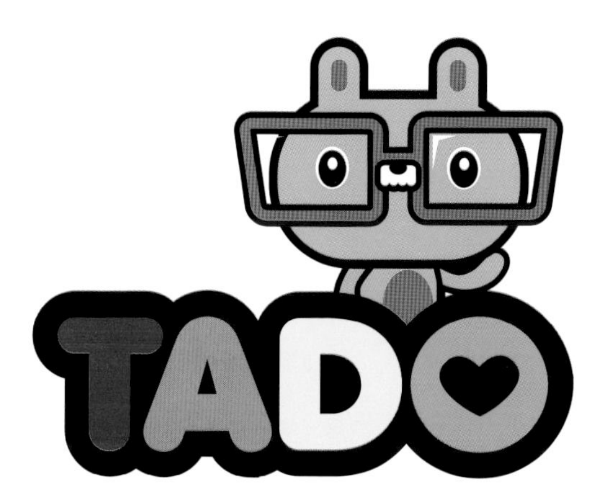

TADO is comprised of Mike Doney and Katie Tang, a couple living and working in Sheffield, UK. Their small studio is the source of adorable characters created to the delight of their clients the world over. TADO loves to embark upon all kinds of projects, everything from publicity, illustrations, fashion, toys, and art exhibitions. TADO's strengths are their little kawaii animals, their great sense of humor, and excellent use of space in their designs. One of the most fascinating things about TADO is that every new project surpasses the popularity of the previous one. This studio's desire to experiment and create is inexhaustible. Not for nothing is this one of the most famous studios in Western kawaii art.

TADO
Sheffield, United Kingdom
www.tado.co.uk
mikeandkatie@tado.co.uk

BIRTHDAY
WISHES!

BIRTHDAY WISHES!

HAPPY BIRTHDA

HAPPY
BIRTHDAY

Private Panda Club

VITAMIN PACK!! 2

p162
BIRTHDAY CARDS
Birthday card designs for 1973
www.nineteenseventythree.com

p163
PRIVATE PANDA
Logo design for the exhibition
The Private Panda Club, 2009
www.privatepandaclub.com
VITAMIN PACK
CD artwork for Universal Music

p164
QUINTEN
Birthday card for a special little person

p165
WILLOW TREE
Wall vinyl produced by Domestic
www.domestic.fr

p166
DOOPERDOO PATTERN
Pattern design for Dooperdoo
2008 clothing range

p167
PANDA LOVE
Artwork for Microsoft's laser-etched
Zune media players

happy day!

super huevón
SUPER CULO
COLACAT
1
2
3
mamáAfrica
YETI
Jamón
ChamusCat

p168
CHARACTERS
Character design

p169
TERELO LOGO

p170
LA CHUMBERA

p171
MR CHOCOLATE
Glacée for the exhibition Battle of the Yeah
Galería Valencia, 2007
www.battleoftheyeah.blogspot.com

Terelo, who is also known as Gazpachan, is one the greatest admirers of kawaii culture in Spain. This was evident by the Puni-Puni exhibition, a show created by a group of Spanish and Japanese artists as a tribute to this delightful art. Terelo's style could be perfectly described as kawaii-folkloric. She herself says that what she likes more is to place herself between stoves and mix the traditional flavors of gazpacho from her birthplace Andalucia, with ingredients from the Japanese kawaii culture. The result amounts to original and exquisite dishes of gastronomic delights packed with characters served in the form of illustrations for magazines, T-shirts, vinyl, amigurumi, etc...

TERELO
Granada, Spain
www.terelo.com
info@terelo.com

la Chumbera

brownie
mr. chocolate

la vez
lo peor
lo mejor

p172
SUPERPOP
Illustration for the magazine *Superpop*

p173
SANDWICH
Illustration for the sex section in the *EP3*
supplement in the *El País* newspaper

SCHOOL
Glacée for the exhibition Mister Pink
Galería Valencia, 2007

PIONONO KING
Glacèe for the exhibition Puni Puni, 2008

tokidoki
latte
....loves me!
....loves me not

p174
© TOKIDOKI, LLC.
Designed by Simone Legno

p175
TOKIDOKI FOR HELLO KITTY PLUSH
© 1976, 2009 SANRIO CO., LTD
© TOKIDOKI, LLC.
Designed by Simone Legno

p176–177
All images on these pages courtesy of Tokidoki
© TOKIDOKI, LLC.
Designed by Simone Legno

From Rome to infinity and beyond. Simone Legno is the tireless artist responsible for the world of Tokidoki. Simone had long endeavored to bring a little of Japan to the rest of the world. Her dream was finally fulfilled when she received an invitation to create his own brand. Simone packed his characters in a suitcase and left for Los Angeles, California. Little can be said of this artist that experts don't already know. Tokidoki is undoubtedly one of the most industrious artists on the kawaii scene. His cache amounts to some tremendously modern graphics, a great deal of sparkle, and a genuine devotion for his work, to which he devotes nearly all of his time.

TOKIDOKI
Los Angeles, USA
www.tokidoki.it

tokidoki
ADIOS
ciao ciao

tokidoki
....loves me!
....loves me not
latte
I LA
www.tokidoki.it

p178–179
TOKIDOKI FOR HELLO KITTY PLUSH

Designed by Simone Legno

p180
MUSIC TOWN

p181
ROLL EGG

Toto Wang presents us with a very personal and surreal interpretation of kawaii art equally in the design of her characters as in their backgrounds and settings. The artist's personal life may have directly impacted the dark nature of her artwork. Toto lost her sight for a short period of time, during which she took refuge in music and her inner world. She heads the Taipei-based No.22. Creative Studio. This studio has also been responsible for all types of merchandising and some very unusual vinyl figures, true to the vision unique to Toto.

TOTO WANG
Taipei, Taiwan
www.ilove22.com
22@ilove22.com

p182
HAPPY SUMMER

p183
TEA FOR LOVE

Tooke

LUCKY

p184–185
TOOKER

p185
LUCKY BUNNY

OR DIE.

p186
GOURMET DE KACHO-FUGETSU

p187
SUSHI BLADE
For the exhibition My Farmicase, 2008

p188–191
GOURMET DE KACHO-FUGETSU

Yukiko Yokoo is a Japanese artist who specializes in graphics for video games. I became enchanted with her art on one of my trips to Japan when I discovered Taiko Drum Master, the most kawaii-influenced video game I have ever seen in my life, designed by Yukiko. Nobody humanizes objects like Yukiko. She says that she likes to combine the traditional Japanese concept of kawaii with pop art. Another of her favorite combinations is that of kawaii and the grotesque, a fusion she refers to as "gro-cute."

YUKIKO YOKOO
Tokyo, Japan
www.bukkoro.com
nya-kuso@bukkoro.com

グルメde花鳥風月

グルメde花鳥風月

グルメde花鳥風月

グルメde花鳥風月

My mother (a bright woman) says good people show their gratitude, so my thanks go out to the following:

To Rubén García and MONSA for their trust in this project from the start.

To Yukari Kawabata for her tremendous help with the Japanese translations. Thank you! Arigatou!

To Pablo Moreno for his great advice and wholehearted support.

To Terelo for helping me to revise the texts and for being so enthusiastic.

To all the artists who have contributed to this book. You have improved my life.

To my family and friends.